International Aid and Integral Human Development

Philip Booth

D1490507

ACTONINSTITUTE

Christian Social Thought Series
Number 16 • Edited by Kevin Schmiesing

Christian Social Thought Series, Number 16

Portions of this monograph have been previously published in *Catholic Social Teaching and the Market Economy*, Hobart Paperback, ed. Philip Booth (London: IEA, 2007). Used with permission.

The author thanks Julian Morris for supplying the figures that appear on page 49.

The Acton Institute acknowledges with gratitude the John Templeton Foundation for its support in the publication of this book.

Cover image: Waiting for school. © Frank van den Bergh
Image from istockphoto.com

ISSN 10: 1-880595-35-4
ISSN 13: 978-1-880595-35-0

ACTONINSTITUTE

98 E. Fulton
Grand Rapids, Michigan 49503
Phone: 616-454-3080
Fax: 616-454-9454
www.acton.org

Printed in the United States of America

Contents

Foreword

A distinctive mark of Christianity from its beginning has been solicitude for the poor. The source of this concern is no mystery: Jesus' own ministry was characterized by compassion toward the marginalized and insistence on the dignity of all people.

With the rise of the contemporary international system of nation-states and the advent of extraordinary economic progress within many of those nations, the Roman Catholic Church recognized a new dimension to its traditional concern for the poor. Perceiving a disturbing imbalance in levels of development among nations, Catholic pastors urged those in richer nations to remember their brothers and sisters abroad.

Identifying an obligation and putting it into practice, however, are two distinct acts. With economists and political leaders, the Church has struggled to understand the mechanics of development and thus to answer the question: How can wealthy nations assist less developed nations in an effective fashion? This apparently simple question is surprisingly difficult to answer.

The most obvious potential solution is for governments of developed nations to transfer funds to governments of developing nations, thus providing resources to create the institutions, services, and infrastructure necessary for economic development. This approach has been attempted and proved unsatisfactory because the dangers of corruption and dependency have attended such aid almost to the point of discrediting it completely.

We should have known better. From the earliest days of the Church, Christians have recognized that material assistance alone is inadequate for the genuine development of the human person. Drawing on this insight, embedded in the social teaching contained in papal encyclicals, financial expert Philip Booth argues that development will never be accomplished merely by "throwing money at the problem." Instead, those concerned about development should take into account the full range of Church teaching on charity, justice, solidarity, and subsidiarity. This approach, more respectful of the dignity and complexity of human nature, can avoid the pitfalls of customary government development aid.

As we enter the second decade of the twenty-first century, the track record of the old model of government assistance is long and clear, as Booth's data substantiate. Led astray by their good intentions, Catholic leaders themselves have sometimes fallen into simplistic recommendations for international aid. Booth urges us to reacquaint ourselves with the rich tradition of the Church's social teaching, examine the economic and other effects of various assistance programs, and creatively refashion our approach to aid. Only in this way will we fulfill our obligation to care for the "least of these," by setting in motion a process of genuine development that leads to prosperity in both material and human goods.

Kevin Schmiesing
Acton Institute

1   Introduction

Of all Christ's teachings as reflected in the gospel accounts, there is none as insistent or as consistent as his defense of the poor and downtrodden. On the strength of this message, the Catholic Church's social teaching has emphasized the Christian's—and indeed all of society's—obligation to assist the poor, and, more broadly, to make use of the gift of wealth in service of the common good. The principles of solidarity, preferential option for the poor, and the universal destination of material goods, have guided the thrust of Catholic social teaching (CST) on this issue.

These principles are relevant not only to domestic policy and individual action at the local level, but also to international relations and individual and societal responsibilities toward the poor and marginalized beyond one's own borders. The Catholic Church, an extensively international body stretching to every corner of the world and profoundly committed to charitable activity in every place to which its influence reaches, has loudly proclaimed the message that developing nations deserve the attention and assistance of the world's richer countries.

The encyclicals of the social tradition have thus served as helpful and necessary reminders of our obligations in charity and justice toward those who exist in a state of dependency. The temptations of apathy and indifference are ever-present and threaten to vitiate the solidarity that CST has rightly promoted as the solution to injustice, instability, and conflict.

Even where there is broad agreement with the principles and aims of CST, the specific approaches and proposals made by Church leaders in the course of their writings on international aid and development remain open to question and debate. Indeed, the Church clearly advises that the applications of its teaching on economic policy are matters for prudential judgment.

To take one example, throughout the CST documents of the past half-century, there has been consistent articulation of the position that the developed world should transfer economic resources to the developing world through government-to-government aid financed by the tax system. The tenor of the teaching has been unambiguous. This teaching has been reflected—indeed magnified and often taken out of context—by local bishops' conferences and Catholic agencies and organizations. This should be, though, a position on which Catholics are free to disagree.

It is easy to see why there might be an inclination toward this position. Certainly, the parable of the Good Samaritan implies that charity should not respect national boundaries; similarly, it could be argued that the use of government aid, financed by taxation, to provide for those in great need or to assist the process of development should not respect national boundaries. However, the argument is less clear with regard to government aid than with regard to charity. If the notion of national sovereignty is to be respected, it may, in practice, be impossible for one country to ensure that the conditions for development are nurtured in another country. Government aid has quite different characteristics from voluntary charity in other respects as well. When examining appropriate policies in relation to government aid, it is important to have an understanding of what does and does not work, underpinned by theoretical and empirical economic examination.

By subjecting the proposals of CST to scrutiny, we will raise important questions. For example, if the provision of aid makes the economic situations of countries worse, if it increases the power of corrupt governments, or if it centralizes power and economic resources rather than disperses power and resources among those in need, how should developed countries respond? It is reasonable for Christians to make a prudential judgment, on the basis of the evidence, that government aid is inappropriate.

Such a conclusion should never apply to voluntary charity. Charity does not bring with it many of the problems of government-provided aid, and it is a serious Christian obligation to help those in poor countries through voluntary sacrifice of time and money.

CST itself exhibits certain tensions that open the door to investigation. The social encyclicals have not ignored the problems that lead to underdeveloped countries being poor, and they have, on occasion, stressed the problems of top-down aid. However, there are statements within CST that seem not to take into account the full economic reality of underdeveloped countries. In particular, it could be argued that insufficient attention has been given to the successful development of many countries without aid. Comparing the performance and policy background within such countries might assist us in developing an appropriate Christian response in these difficult areas.

This more fruitful response, too, draws on the resources of CST. The principle of subsidiarity warns against the dangers of large institutional efforts to combat problems that are essentially local and impervious to grand schemes. Perhaps popes and bishops have not always applied the lesson of subsidiarity as vigorously as they should when assessing the likely result of recommended approaches to fostering the development of poor nations. With a fuller appreciation of the economics of development, of the history of successful development, and of the effects of government-to-government aid, Catholic leaders will be better able to apply the principles of the social teaching in ways that further the goal of genuine human development for all people.

II True Development

Most secular discussion of aid and development implicitly assumes that development involves a movement toward economic prosperity and the production and consumption of material goods. While this is sometimes qualified by highlighting provision for basic health care and a desire to improve life expectancy, the basic poverty benchmarks relate to material living standards. Indeed, services such as health and education are often regarded as important because they are seen as a path to material prosperity. In this context, aid is generally thought of as a means of lifting people out of material poverty—or, at least, the provision of assistance to help people lift themselves out of material poverty.

Clearly, development in a Christian context also has an economic aspect. Catholic social teaching is oriented toward the promotion of the *common good*, and this requires that the conditions for human flourishing, for people to "reach their fulfillment more fully and easily," exist (GS, no. 26).[1] This, in turn, requires the availability of certain goods and services such as clean water, adequate food, basic education, shelter, and health care. While the main focus of our discussion will be on such economic aspects of development, it is important to note two qualifications. The first is that economic development

---

[1]   A list of abbreviations of Church documents appears at the end of this text.

is but one aspect—and not the most important—of human development. A fuller concept of development—what Pope Benedict calls *integral human development*—understands true human fulfillment to come through spiritual progress, an achievement to which material development acts in service.

The second point is that development should take place in the context of a people living out objective moral truths. This is a theme that is stressed in *Caritas in Veritate*, discussed below. As such, for example, the Church would not regard it as valid to use artificial methods of population control, even if it could be shown that such methods brought about higher material living standards or a lower level of dire poverty.[2]

Father Rodger Charles, SJ, summarizes the idea of true development effectively, based on an understanding of two encyclicals, *Populorum Progressio* and *Sollicitudo Rei Socialis*. The main features, he argues, are these: true development must be moral; people should not become slaves to consumer goods through overdevelopment; people must be free to own property and save; cultural identity and openness to God must be respected; the rights of the person—including young, old, and those of all political views—must be respected; development must also respect the natural world.[3]

It should be said that there is no conflict between true development as defined by the Church and the set of conditions that most economists believe should exist if there is to be material development. However, understanding material development in the wider context of true development is an important check on those who may define development too narrowly. True development is compatible with various political systems, but it is not compatible, for example, with systems in which those with particular political or religious beliefs are oppressed. Countries

---

[2] There is in fact little evidence to show that population control is a cause of economic growth, though this particular issue will not be pursued further in this monograph.

[3] Rodger Charles, SJ, *Christian Social Witness and Teaching: The Catholic Tradition from Genesis to Centesimus Annus* (Leominster, UK: Gracewing, 1998), 335–37.

that have managed material development while practicing such oppression are not to be admired. We may be able to learn something from those regimes that have reduced absolute poverty while neglecting other aspects of development, and the reduction in absolute poverty is certainly a consolation. However, we should ensure that the other aspects of true development are not neglected by countries whose governments have achieved reductions in poverty while preventing, sometimes brutally, other aspects of the development of the human person. At the same time, we should not be comfortable with regimes that allow political participation in democracy if economic freedom is not permitted and economic development cannot take place.

With these important qualifications in place, we will outline CST's treatment of the economic dimension of development and examine how it can be applied to the circumstances of the twenty-first century.

III   Charity or Aid?

Solidarity, Universal Destination, and Preferential Option

The Christian desire to assist the economic development of poorer peoples is founded on the principles of solidarity, the universal destination of material goods, and the preferential option for the poor.

John Paul II defined solidarity as "a firm and persevering determination to commit oneself to the common good; that is to say, to the good of all and of each individual" (SRS, no. 38). As human persons, we are members of the human community, encompassing all other human persons. Although our more direct and immediate responsibilities involve those closest to us, we are obliged to act in ways that promote the good also of all of those who comprise this human community.

The principle of the universal destination of goods stems from Christian theology's understanding of God's beneficent creation. "God intended the earth with everything contained in it for the use of all human beings and peoples" (GS, no. 69). The material wealth of the created world should not be restricted to the benefit of a few; it is designed to be shared and redound to the good of all human beings. It must be noted that this principle is not at odds with CST's vigorous defense of the institution of private property. The holding of property by individuals is the normal channel through which the universal destination of goods is served. Property rights are in no way vitiated by this teaching, but they are held to entail certain limitations and obligations—expressed in part by the ideas of solidarity and preferential option for the poor (see CA, no. 30).

The preferential option for the poor is a reflection of the Christian Church's longstanding solicitude for the defenseless and marginalized, stretching back to the earliest days of Christianity and to the life of Christ himself. "It is proper," Pope John XXIII wrote, "that the duty of helping the poor and unfortunate should especially stir Catholics, since they are members of the Mystical Body of Christ" (MM, no. 159). The preferential option should not be seen as an invitation to injustice—treating one group or another as any more or less deserving of dignity and protection—but as a recognition of the reality that the wealthy and well-connected are better able to defend their own interests and to meet their own needs than are the poor and marginalized. Thus the Church urges its people to pay close attention to those who are too easily ignored or forgotten.

These principles together represent a formidable exhortation to Catholics to assist those in need. In its international dimension, this means especially providing support to the citizens of nations that are mired in poverty and whose economic progress lags behind that of the developed world. All three principles are rooted in and are expressions of the principle at the heart of the Christian life: love. To be concerned about and act in favor of the poor around the world is to practice the virtue of charity.

However, in this context, it is a mistake to equate charity with government aid. When the Church talks about solidarity and the preferential option, it usually refers to these concepts in the context of charity: the service of love in providing for one's neighbor without expecting anything in return. In his 2009 World Peace Day message, for example, Pope Benedict XVI said: "[I]t is timely to recall in particular the 'preferential love for the poor' in the light of the primacy of charity, which is attested throughout the Christian tradition, beginning with that of the early Church."[4]

Indeed, solidarity is a virtue to be practiced in our daily lives and requires sacrifice. As has been noted, it is not something that can be delegated to government. Still less does voting for a political party that will tax the rich people up the road to send money to the (possibly despotic) governments of poor people in a different part of the world discharge our obligations in solidarity.

This is not to say that there is no role for governments in providing aid for poor nations. However, such aid does not fulfill our duty of solidarity, and it is for individual Christians to make prudential judgments as to whether government aid is effective in aiding the poor. That government provision of any good, service, or assistance does not discharge our duties and cannot bring the world to perfection was made clear by Pope Benedict XVI: "There is no ordering of the State so just that it can eliminate the need for a service of love. Whoever wants to eliminate love is preparing to eliminate man as such. There will always be suffering which cries out for consolation and help" (DCE, no. 28b).

Indeed, one cannot stress too strongly the difference between a service of love and charity combined with the virtue of solidarity, on the one hand, and government-to-government aid transfers, on the other.

The Distinction Between Charity and Aid

In the tradition of Catholic social teaching, a preference is generally expressed for voluntary action to help the poor over coercive means such as the use of taxation. It is worth exploring further this important distinction between government provision of aid and charity because so many of the confusions in the

---

[4] "Fighting Poverty to Build Peace," Message of His Holiness Pope Benedict XVI for the Celebration of the World Day of Peace 2009, no. 15. Available at www. vatican.va.

aid debate arise as a result of campaigners moving seamlessly from the Christian requirement to choose to help the poor using one's own resources to a supposed requirement to help the poor using resources taken from others in the form of taxation. Indeed, many people today discuss taxation in the same terms as they discuss charity, as if taxation were simply an extension of charitable giving. Words such as *generous* and *compassionate*, which can only relate to voluntary sacrifice, are often used to describe the actions of government redistributing income to achieve particular ends through taxation. As we have already seen, however, Church teaching makes clear the difference between charity and action taken through political structures.

Those differences are many. They include the fact that charitable giving is a genuine act of love whereas taxation is coercive: There is no choice exercised by the taxpayer and therefore no generosity or compassion is possible. Taxation is impersonal in that it cannot be used to address the concerns of the taxpayer, and the payer of taxes cannot develop a personal relationship with the recipient. The ends to which taxes are put are determined through preferences expressed by lobbying through the political system. If the state takes the primary role in this respect, then people cannot use their own talents and resources in their own way, guided by the will of God, to relieve the suffering of others. Quite simply, state redistribution through political structures is not an extension of charity but an alternative and different mechanism for the allocation of resources from that of voluntary initiative.

These differences are well understood in Church teaching. Pope Leo XIII in *Rerum Novarum* proposed the use of coercive redistribution using political structures only after genuine acts of love, expressed through the charitable giving of money and time, have failed to make the necessary provision. Leo judged that the giving of alms is not a duty of justice, except in extreme cases, but of Christian charity: "a duty not enforced by human law" (RN, no. 22).

Pope Benedict XVI discussed some of these issues in *Deus Caritas Est*. He expressed the view that charity is a manifestation of love as well as a Christian duty that is inseparable from other aspects of the Church's mission. Charity involves an outpouring of love that combines material help with genuine personal concern. Pope Benedict confirms the message of John Paul II's *Centesimus Annus* that a state that tried to provide for all material need would become a mere bureaucracy. He also notes that the needs of the poor are not just material and that, even in the most just state, charity would be necessary, for charity meets needs in a way that is more fully human than the way that a state must meet them (see CA, no. 48 and DCE, no. 28b). In *Caritas in Veritate* (no. 38), Pope Benedict repeats the sentiments of *Sollicitudo Rei Socialis* when he writes: "Solidarity is first and foremost a sense of responsibility on the part of everyone with regard to everyone, and it cannot therefore be merely delegated to the State."

Charity can also be undermined by state action. This can happen in several ways. As the state undertakes functions that properly belong in the community or under the auspices of charity, its bureaucratic methods can prevent others from helping those who are in need of charity. This has been a problem for some years in the United Kingdom, where the state has been hostile to charities with a Christian ethic. Furthermore, state action financially crowds out charitable giving. If fifty cents of every dollar earned is taken by the state, as is the case in many Western countries, it is harder for individuals to meet their own basic needs, to act for the good of themselves and their families, and to contribute toward meeting the needs of others through charity. All this is not to deny a legitimate role for the state, but, in the Christian mind, that role should be subservient to solutions to the problems of poverty that involve the exercise of true Christian love.

Where, therefore, might the case for tax-financed aid exist? Nicholas Townsend has expressed quite succinctly where the role of the state may become important.[5] Political authorities play their part in bringing about the common good. To do this, they set the framework of laws within which individuals, families, and communities operate. It is not the state's role to correct all moral wrongs (we would not expect the state take legal action against all people who lied in personal relationships, for example). However, the state may enact laws to stop people from committing wrongs that prevent others from participating in the common good (prohibiting murder and theft, for example). Townsend goes on to point out that the state may also enact laws where sins of omission are of sufficient seriousness to prevent people from participating in the common good. Thus if charity is not sufficiently generous to allow people to have the basics of life (such as food, clean water, and health care) the state may step in. It may do this on an international basis if the capacity of individual national states is insufficient. The state may also provide certain infrastructure that is necessary to promote the common good.

This approach is clearly compatible with the thinking of Pope Leo in *Rerum Novarum*, and with the principle of subsidiarity articulated first by Pope Pius XI in *Quadragesimo Anno* (1931) and reiterated by subsequent popes, including John Paul II:

> A community of a higher order should not interfere in the internal life of a community of a lower order, depriving the latter of its functions, but rather should support it in case of need and help to coordinate its activity with the activities of the rest of society, always with a view to the common good (CA, no. 48).

However, it also leaves a wide area for judgment in four respects. First, if government aid actually does more harm than good, it would be imprudent to use aid to try to promote the common good. Though it might be thought that sending aid can only help the population of poor countries have the basics

---

[5]   Nicholas Townsend, "Government and Social Infrastructure: A Fourth Way," in *God and Government*, ed. J. Chaplin and N. Spencer (London: SPCK, 2009).

they need to thrive, paradoxically this may not be the case, as will be discussed below. Second, we may wish to use government policy to encourage more voluntary support.[6] Third, there is the question of how much aid should be provided and how it should be delivered. Finally, especially if it is shown that aid does not raise the living standards of a recipient country, we may wish to pursue other policies to try to bring about long-term and fruitful change in the political and economic character of a country.

Given this latitude within the Church's teaching, and given the evidence below, Christian leaders should be careful in their exhortations to others, particularly those for whom they have pastoral responsibility, and in their comments in the political arena regarding this subject. Urging Christians and all people of good will to be generous toward the poor is part and parcel of the pastor's responsibility as a teacher of truth, but specifying how that obligation applies in the political sphere involves one or more steps of translation of principle into action. That the Church does not claim special knowledge in the fields where expertise is necessary in this process implies that any such policy recommendations should be presented with circumspection and with care to highlight the distinction between the social doctrine and matters of prudential judgment.

---

[6] For example, charitable assistance to underdeveloped countries is about ten times greater in the United States than in France, partly because of the generous way in which charitable assistance is treated in the U.S. tax system.

IV Catholic Social Teaching: Making the Case for Aid

Exhortation to Provide Foreign Aid

As noted above, the Church's commitment to solidarity among all people of the world leads it to promote the development of poorer nations. This obligation is first and foremost an individual responsibility to exercise charity, but it also has a social dimension. Pope John Paul II states: "The obligation to commit oneself to the development of peoples is not just an individual duty, and still less an individualistic one, as if it were possible to achieve this development through the isolated efforts of each individual. It is an imperative which obliges each and every man and woman, as well as societies and nations" (SRS, no. 32). He also insists that solidarity should not recognize international borders (SRS, no. 39). This international vision of the principle of solidarity is rooted in the parable of the Good Samaritan in which recognition of the obligations of a common humanity overcome prejudices based on ethnic or religious divisions.

The Second Vatican Council's constitution, *Gaudium et Spes*, similarly emphasized the need to see solidarity in global terms. The council fathers expressed concern about inequalities in economic outcomes: "excessive economic and social differences between the members of one human family or population groups cause scandal and militate against social justice..." (no. 29). Chapter 2 of part 1 finishes with the statement that "solidarity must be constantly increased until that day on which it will be brought to perfection" (no. 32).

It is important to note that these passages do not necessarily describe a solidarity promoted through political structures. *Gaudium et Spes* recognizes the importance of fostering the conditions necessary for homegrown development: "technical progress, an inventive spirit, an eagerness to create and to expand enterprises ... all the elements of development must be promoted" (no. 64). That the Church does not envisage a state-directed system is clear in *Gaudium et Spes*' criticism of collective organization of production (no. 65). The document also criticizes political systems that do not foster private property and sound money and promote the virtues of what today would be called good governance.

At once recognizing the clear distinction between the provision of development assistance through charity and its provision through tax-financed aid as well as CST's eschewing of government domination of the economy, it is nonetheless true that the same documents at times explicitly favor government action through development aid. *Gaudium et Spes* (no. 69) makes it clear that both individuals and governments should share their goods to relieve suffering and to help peoples to develop themselves. In paragraph 84, it stresses the importance of international organizations in fostering development.

Populorum Progressio (Pope Paul VI, 1967) expanded the analysis of *Rerum Novarum* to apply it to world problems, particularly those of development. As in *Gaudium et Spes*, Pope Paul spells out conditions of good governance and the conditions for development. He emphasizes the importance of private property and free competition and criticizes planned and collectivized economies. However, he also explicitly promotes aid as an agenda for governments rather than merely an activity of charity. Nations as well as individuals are told that they most partake in the process of building solidarity. People are told that they must accept higher taxes to finance distributions to poorer countries. *Populorum Progressio* proposes an increased role for international institutions, particularly the United Nations. Development is described as a "right," which imposes a duty on all nations—both developed and underdeveloped.

There seems to be a detectable shift from *Gaudium et Spes* to *Populorum Progressio*. Overall, *Gaudium et Spes* offers a mature discussion of the problem of the poorest in underdeveloped countries. The conditions for indigenous growth are understood, responsibility of Christian groups is made clear, development as primarily the responsibility of people themselves is made clear, and conditions necessary for long-term development are understood and effectively articulated. *Populorum Progressio* appears in contrast to have been influenced to a greater degree by the fashions of development economists in the 1960s. It was certainly influenced by Pope Paul's own experience visiting the then-impoverished nation of India.[7] In both documents there is, however, a responsibility put on the governments of developed countries and on international organizations (generally financed by developed countries) to furnish aid both for relief and for development.

An important lacuna in these documents' discussion of development aid is an exposition of the negative effects that government aid may produce on the receiving nation. Again, this is a function of their historical context: Studies documenting this dark side of the aid picture have increased exponentially in the decades since *Populorum Progressio* was published. In particular, there is ample evidence that granting aid to countries in which the conditions of good governance do not exist could actually do harm, a problem that we consider in more detail below. This observation is interesting, given the context of *Populorum Progressio*, as India is possibly one of the best examples of a country that failed to develop because of policies both of poor governance and of central planning.

It is reasonable for a Christian to suggest that aid should be granted to countries if the aid benefits the poorest, or even if

---

[7]   Charles, *Christian Social Witness*, 232.

it does no harm. However, the question remains: What happens if government-to-government aid, of the type proposed by *Populorum Progressio*, actually acts to strengthen the institutions that have brought about the failure to develop in the first place?

More Nuanced Discussions of Aid

More recent Church documents, while often continuing to recommend government aid, seem to have taken the historical record of the effectiveness of aid into account, thus producing a more nuanced discussion. There has been more emphasis on expressing solidarity through private charity, and the responsibilities of developing countries have been given at least equal, if not greater, weight than the role of developed nations.

The *Catechism of the Catholic Church* (1994) makes a distinction between the provision of aid to address particular problems and assistance given for development: "Direct aid is an appropriate response to immediate, extraordinary needs caused by natural catastrophes, epidemics, and the like. But it does not suffice to repair the grave damage resulting from destitution or to provide a lasting solution to a country's needs" (no. 2440). To achieve the latter, it argues, requires reform of institutions.

In addition, the Catechism emphasizes the integral character of development: it is necessary to ensure that development is both spiritual and material. It states: "Rich nations have a grave moral responsibility towards those which are *unable* to ensure the means of their development by themselves or have been prevented from doing so by tragic historical events" (no. 2439, italics added). Of course, this may include those who are prevented from prospering as a result of the policies of their own governments but, once again, it emphasizes the importance of personal responsibility for development, where individuals are allowed to take such responsibility.

Caritas in Veritate is the most recent major papal statement on social questions. Before being delayed, it was intended that the document would be published around the fortieth anniversary of *Populorum Progressio*. As such, there is a strong emphasis on the development of the world's poorest countries. The word *aid* is mentioned 19 times and the word *development* over 250 times. The underlying message is that matters of development and justice cannot be separated from moral truths relating to the nature of the human person. Thus, it focuses strongly on economic development only as part of *integral human development*, as discussed above.

That Pope Benedict has not abandoned papal exhortations to governments to provide aid is clear. The encyclical states: "economically developed nations should do all they can to allocate larger portions of their gross domestic product to development aid" (no. 60). This passage must be read in context, however. It is the only point in the encyclical where more aid or this type of aid is explicitly recommended. On fifteen of the nineteen occasions on which the word *aid* is used, the Holy Father is critical of aid agencies, the way in which Western governments provide aid, or of the way in which recipient governments use aid.

Benedict writes: "International aid has often been diverted from its proper ends, through irresponsible actions" (CV, no. 22). He reminds us of the "grave irresponsibility of the governments of former colonies." Presciently, the pope also tells us how we can avoid these problems. For example, he says: "Aid programs must increasingly acquire the characteristics of participation and completion from the grass roots" (no. 58). In other words, we do not discharge our responsibilities simply when we provide aid (whether through charity or government transfers). Those responsible have a duty—a very serious duty given the historical record—to ensure that aid is provided in a bottom-up way that genuinely leads to development for the poor.

The pope also stresses the importance of "institution building" for development (e.g., no. 41). John Paul II outlined certain important roles for the state in *Centesimus Annus*, and Benedict's encyclical reflects this approach, seemingly taking on board the lessons from those modern schools of economics—which also reflect classical economic thinking—that stress the importance of good institutions of governance for development. *Caritas* suggests that a main focus of development aid should be to ensure that institutions exist so that the rule of law, protection of property rights, a properly functioning democracy, proper systems for maintaining public order, and so on, all thrive. "The focus of *international aid*, within a solidarity-based plan to resolve today's economic problems," it states, "should rather be on consolidating constitutional, juridical and administrative systems in countries that do not yet fully enjoy these goods" (CV, no. 41). As if to anticipate the accusation that promoting such institution building amounts to "cultural imperialism," the pope points out that this basic framework, within which the economy and civil society develop, will reflect the specific culture within which it is embedded.

Benedict criticizes tied aid (assistance that must be spent in the nation providing it) and warns about aid dependency; he also demands a removal of developed-country trade barriers, which stop underdeveloped countries from selling their goods and produce. Indeed, he links the two points and suggests, in keeping with the tradition of Catholic social teaching, that aid should be temporary and that trade is the "principal form of assistance" to be provided to underdeveloped countries. In other words, countries should not be dependent on aid but move away from aid toward self-supporting economies:

> Such aid, whatever the donors' intentions, can some-times lock people into a state of dependence and even foster situations of localized oppression and exploita-tion in the receiving country. Economic aid, in order to be true to its purpose, must not pursue secondary objectives.... It should also be remembered that, in the economic sphere, the principal form of assistance needed by developing countries is that of allowing and encouraging the gradual penetration of their products into international markets, thus making it possible for these countries to participate fully in international economic life (no. 58).

Caritas also has advice for those involved in distributing aid, including agencies and charities. As the pope says: "International organizations might question the actual effectiveness of their bureaucratic and administrative machinery, which is often excessively costly" (no. 47). He calls for complete financial transparency for all aid organizations. He blames both providers of aid and recipients for diverting money from the purposes for which it was intended. He expresses concern that aid can lead to dependence and also, if badly administered, can give rise to exploitation and oppression. This can happen where aid budgets are large in relation to developing countries' domestic budgets and the money gets into the hands of the rich and powerful rather than the poor and needy.

While these discussions are very important, the main message of the encyclical is not economic or political. The key theme, reiterated throughout the document, is that development requires the correct moral orientation: Charity cannot be separated from the pursuit of truth. For example, the pope says: "Some non-governmental organizations work actively to spread abortion.... Moreover, there is reason to suspect that development aid is sometimes linked to specific health-care policies which de facto involve the imposition of strong birth control measures" (CV, no. 28). He comments that openness to life is at the center of true development. Any development approach or program that fails to recognize the moral dimension is deficient and potentially counterproductive.

Pope John Paul II had discussed the problem of providing aid where there are imperfect political structures, but the implications were less fully drawn out than they have been by Pope Benedict. For example, John Paul stated that extreme poverty in underdeveloped countries happens, "not through the fault of the needy people, and even less through a sort of inevitability dependent on natural conditions or circumstances as a whole" (SRS, no. 9). More specifically, John Paul referred to "grave instances of omissions on the part of developing nations themselves, and especially on the part of those holding economic and political power" as being responsible for the deterioration in the position of underdeveloped countries (SRS, no. 16). He went on to mention the problem of aid that is misused: "... investments and aid for development are often diverted from their proper purpose and used to sustain conflicts" (SRS, no. 21). However, the accent here is not on misuse due to internal decisions but as a result of directions from donors, particularly in the context of the Cold War. As Benedict observes in *Caritas*, such misuse of aid did not stop when the Cold War ended.

John Paul then further examined the background in which development assistance is given. He commented on the structures of social sin, rooted in individual sin, that cause underdevelopment. Again, however, many of the problems identified relate to donor communities rather than the political systems of recipient countries—still reflecting the Cold War period when aid was often used as a tool to obtain political influence. However, some responsibility is thrust on the leaders and peoples of developing countries: "Development demands above all a spirit of initiative on the part of the countries which need it" (SRS, no. 44). "Other nations need to reform certain unjust structures, and in particular their political institutions, in order to replace corrupt, dictatorial and authoritarian forms of government by democratic and participatory ones" (SRS, no. 44). There is a clear emphasis in this document on creating the economic conditions to allow growth and development to take place, rather than on the transfer of economic resources through aid.

The importance of the wider institutional background necessary for economic development and prosperity is stated clearly in the Catechism, which reaffirms the message of *Centesimus Annus*:

> The activity of a market economy cannot be conducted in an institutional, juridical or political vacuum. On the contrary, it presupposes sure guarantees of individual freedom and private property, as well as a stable currency and efficient public services. Hence the principal task of the state is to guarantee this security, so that

> those who work and produce can enjoy the fruits of their labors and thus feel encouraged to work efficiently and honestly ..." (CCC, no. 2431)

Thus, it is clear that the Church has not ignored the institutional and political requirements that are necessary for economic development and prosperity and, in recent years, has given them greater emphasis. Indeed, *Centesimus Annus* goes further in making clear that those countries that *have* developed are those that have participated in "international economic activities" (i.e., trade in goods, services, and capital). This is an important move forward and change of emphasis from the encyclicals of the 1960s, which tended to stress income transfers.

This analysis leaves open, however, the issue of how we should respond if the political, legal, and economic environment is not only hostile to economic development but also such that aid will be wasted and may be used to centralize power within corrupt political systems. The existence of this possibility should at least make us hesitate before calling automatically for increased aid either to promote development or to help those on low incomes in underdeveloped countries. Aid, in the wrong political environment, might do significant harm. Even *Caritas in Veritate* did not broach the question of how we should respond if aid actually entrenches the conditions that militate against economic development. If advocates of CST are to promote effectively the integral human development that the encyclicals endorse, then it is critical to conduct a realistic assessment of the impact of aid in these difficult national environments. We will take up the task in chapter 6.

Aid, Catholic Agencies, and Local Bishops' Conferences

The message in the social encyclicals is delivered with compassion and wisdom. Although some economists may regard various specific pieces of advice as misguided in light of economic reality, the encyclicals operate in a wider context that leaves the reader sure that political proselytizing is not the aim of the documents. The difficulties and limitations of development aid are generally understood and communicated, even if these are not the aspects of the teaching that is most well known.

The same cannot always be said for documents generated by local bishops' conferences or by Catholic agencies. There is sometimes little self-doubt and little qualification apparent in the statements that are made. Subjective policy prescriptions are proposed as if they are objective matters. There seems to be little awareness of the distinction between charitable actions and government-to-government aid or admission that, depending on the circumstances, aid can be harmful.

For example, CAFOD, the major British Catholic aid agency, issued a guide for the United Kingdom's 2010 general election in which it stated:

> Our faith calls us to share what we have with those in need. Aid that is well targeted and well-managed can make an enormous difference to people in poverty… but there's not enough of it. In 1970, rich countries at the United Nations pledged to give 0.7 per cent of their national income in aid. Today, only a handful of countries have met this target although some are working towards it.[8]

This statement moves seamlessly from an invocation of charity (sharing what we have) to an endorsement of government-to-government aid (sharing what other people have) and goes on to implicitly advocate the specific proposal that political parties should promise to turn the 0.7 percent aid pledge into law.

This type of statement leads to confusion concerning the character of the Church's teaching on development as we have described it. While it is plausible to argue that solidarity implies a state-level commitment to aid other states, the one does not necessarily follow from the other. As we have pointed out, any such endorsement must at the least take into account

---

[8] CAFOD, *Your Guide to the 2010 General Election* (London: CAFOD, n.d.).

local circumstances and thus be hedged with qualifications. It should also emphasize the priority of individual responsibility to act in charity. Advocating a specific level of government aid, moreover, takes the application of solidarity and the preferential option for the poor to a level further removed from the inarguable principles of CST. Whenever Catholic leaders make such arguments, it is advisable that they stipulate that their policy recommendations are distinct from authoritative Church teaching.

One temptation that Catholic agencies confront is that of equating Church teaching with the agencies' own self-interest. Grants from government aid budgets, for example, comprise a significant proportion of CAFOD's own income: they now equal an amount equivalent to 30 percent of private donations. This of itself is not necessarily a bad thing. Aid money is arguably better spent when it is directed through charities than when it is delivered directly by government bureaucracies. Nevertheless, this is a potentially dangerous situation. The easiest way for an agency to increase its resources may well be by campaigning for increased government aid budgets and through parliamentary lobbying rather than through developing the unconditional charity that individual Catholic supporters provide. Given this, it is worth noting that CAFOD's spending on "education and campaigns" in 2008–2009 was about ten times the total annual donations to the Institute of Economic Affairs (IEA), a major British policy and education think tank covering all areas of economics. CAFOD thus devotes substantial resources to campaigning and otherwise promoting the case for increased aid or government intervention in other respects.

The bishops of the United States, through their national organization, the United States Conference of Catholic Bishops (USCCB), have given similarly unconditional support for government development aid. Their 2009 document, *Questions on Church Teaching and International Assistance* would appear to be their definitive statement on the subject of external aid, though it is a short document.

The authors deserve praise for their attention to moral issues related to international development. They write, for example, that the USCCB "works vigorously to preserve barriers to U.S. funds being used to promote abortion." Regrettably, the document's transition from the morality to the economics of aid exhibits familiar weaknesses.

After describing aid as a "moral responsibility," the document then moves on to pose and answer the question: What has international assistance helped to accomplish? Here, it cites a fall in the number of the world's very poor by 400 million. Economic evidence will be discussed in more detail below, but one example here will suffice to make the point that this asserted connection between aid and a decline in poverty is extremely doubtful. Estimates of the size of the fall in the number of very poor in China over the last two decades or so range from about 250 million to 400 million, and other Asian countries such as Vietnam have also seen astonishing declines in absolute poverty. Such Asian countries account for the greatest share of the reduction in absolute poverty in recent years, yet they are not among the top thirty recipients of U.S. foreign aid between 1996 and 2006. There is no evidence that government aid has made a significant contribution to the material progress of developing nations.

The advice that the USCCB has given before elections has been of a similar style. Its 2004 election document is notable and the relevant section was repeated verbatim in 2008. In these documents, it is stated that the United States should take a leading role in helping to alleviate global poverty through a comprehensive development agenda, including substantially increased development aid for the poorest countries.[9] Interestingly, in the introductory section, the 2008 document stressed the complementary roles of laity and clergy and pointed

---

[9]   See http://www.usccb.org/faithfulcitizenship/faithfulcitizenship03.pdf for the 2004 election document and http://www.usccb.org/faithfulcitizenship/FCStatement.pdf for the 2008 document.

out that clergy should merely state the fundamental moral principles. Yet, the remainder of the document is laced with specific policy proposals!

The bishops of England and Wales have also generally taken a stance that supports foreign aid. CAFOD, referred to above, is ultimately answerable to the bishops' conference. However, the bishops' 2010 pre-election document was very sober and, with a few exceptions, did limit itself to stating the principles that Catholics should bear in mind when voting on certain issues. Specifically, on the issue of foreign aid, it said: "The community to which the principle of the common good applies extends globally and includes future generations. This requires that we all face up to our responsibilities for international aid and development." Of course, Christians must face up to their responsibilities. This must involve prudential judgment—including whether or not to support the provision of government-to-government foreign aid. The bishops of England and Wales pitched this statement exactly as it should have been.

In general, though, it is difficult in bishops' conference or Catholic aid agency pronouncements to find qualifications of the case for the provision of government aid or criticisms of underdeveloped country governance of the style that are found in *Caritas in Veritate*. To the contrary, there are frequent definitive statements about the provision of foreign aid without any questions being expressed over whether foreign aid has done more harm than good. This is a pity because it gives the impression that the authors do not fully understand the issues at stake. As such, they lay themselves open to criticism from economists working in the field as well as to exploitation by special interests and politicians who may not share the Church's aims.

V Underlying Economic Assumptions

Some of the debatable recommendations offered in Church documents appear to be based on mistaken observations of economic reality. These observations become the premises for misguided applications of the principles of CST. By examining these premises and furnishing more accurate information concerning the actual economic situations being confronted, we hope to suggest more fruitful avenues of action for Catholics who are determined to address the pressing needs of those who suffer from material deprivation.

One crucial premise that is detectable in many documents is that poverty is rising and inequality growing. At the very least, one can say that the great achievements in terms of reducing poverty of recent years have not been fully recognized. Perhaps this is the case because those achievements have, in the main, taken place outside predominantly Catholic countries and have also taken place in countries that have not received significant amounts of development aid.

This false premise is articulated, for example, in the *Compendium of the Social Doctrine*: "In fact, there are indications aplenty that point to a trend of *increasing inequalities*, both between advanced countries and developing countries, and within industrialized countries. The growing economic wealth made possible by the processes [of globalization] ... is accompanied by an increase in relative poverty."[10] In *Populorum Progressio*, Pope Paul VI stated that "the poor nations remain ever poorer while the rich ones become still richer" (PP, no. 57). John Paul II speaks of, "hopes for development, at that time [at the time of *Populorum Progressio*, 1967] so lively, today appear very far from being realized" (SRS, no. 12) and adds, "the first negative observation to make is the persistence and often widening of the gap between the areas of the so-called developed North and the developing South" (SRS, no. 14).

While they cannot be labeled completely inaccurate, statements such as these are simplistic and misleading. It is true that there are certain countries, sometimes described as "failed states" that have not shared in the economic growth arising from globalization because they have not participated in the process of globalization.[11] As other countries have grown richer, partly as a result of globalization, people in failed states whose incomes have only grown slowly, or have perhaps shrunk, become relatively poorer. This arises because of the failure of such states to reap the benefits of international trade—not because of inherent faults in the process of globalization. This point is certainly not recognized in the *Compendium*, which, quoting from the encyclicals of John Paul II, explicitly suggests that countries are being left behind *as a result of* globalization.

It is also worth noting that the *Compendium* focuses, in the statement above, on *relative* poverty. The emphasis on relative poverty in the *Compendium* seems inappropriate. Catholic social teaching has generally emphasized meeting basic needs as the motivation for charity and government intervention. The common good requires ensuring that the conditions exist for human flourishing for all. As such, the reduction of relative poverty would appear to be a misplaced aim because it wrongly shifts the focus from a genuine problem (absolute poverty) to

---

[10] *Compendium of the Social Doctrine of the Church* (Rome: Pontifical Council for Justice and Peace, 2005), no. 362, italics in original; hereafter *Compendium*.

[11] See Martin Wolf, *Why Globalization Works* (New Haven, Conn.: Yale University Press, 2004).

a phenomenon that in many cases may not be a problem at all. If, for example, some communities wish to partake in economic development only until a point at which basic needs are met but go no further, then while the rest of the world becomes richer, that country's relative poverty will increase.[12] This "relative poverty," voluntarily chosen, is not a marker of injustice crying out for amelioration. In fact, the concept of relative poverty is problematic because it can be difficult to differentiate it from inequality of income per se. Yet, the Church has never condemned economic inequality in principle. In a market system, some such inequality is inevitable. Some people will choose to work longer hours or at occupations that are more difficult or that require skilled training. These people will naturally acquire material goods at a rate faster than others. Far from representing an unjust system, this result is a just effect of the expression of human freedom.

A second way that a focus on relative poverty is misplaced is that it can distract us from genuine problems and misdirect attention to innocent developments. For example, if a large part of the world's population were able to meet basic needs as a result of globalization (whereas they could not do so before) but, at the same time, other countries were able to become richer still, then it is possible for relative poverty to increase. This will not call into question globalization as a source of material enhancement to humankind in general. The culprit here would not be globalization; it would be whatever factors were slowing down economic development in the lagging nations—most likely failures of government to provide the conditions necessary for the unleashing of the creative potential of the country's human and natural resources.

Finally, the notion of relative poverty is dangerous because focusing undue attention on it easily leads to the vice of envy.

---

[12] I refer here to a situation of voluntary choice of individuals and groups of individuals. People in religious orders are, of course, the most obvious example. However, there may be other communities whose members freely choose a simpler way of life.

While CST has made clear that all human beings deserve to possess the basic material necessities to permit them to fulfill their potential as human persons, it does not insist that material goods be evenly distributed across society. By emphasizing relative poverty, we run the risk of encouraging individuals to measure their living standards by comparison with others.

Yet, even the foregoing is a really hypothetical discussion that has not taken into account what has actually occurred in recent world history. As it happens, fortunately, relative poverty has decreased during the process of globalization, and absolute poverty has decreased dramatically. Most strikingly, the gap between countries that have recently seen rapid growth and those countries that have been relatively well off for many decades has narrowed significantly. Stylized facts do not prove the point, but they provide sufficient information to seriously question the premise that globalization is leaving the poor behind. In China, three hundred million people have been pulled out of "dollar-a-day" poverty in the last decade. It is inconceivable that this would have happened without China's participation in the process of globalization. The same could well happen in India in the next decade if India continues to liberalize its economy and allows trade to develop.

More broadly, the income of poor countries has not, in general, grown more slowly than that of rich countries during the recent episode of globalization. For example, India, Sri Lanka, China, Chile, and Pakistan have all grown faster than the world average over the last ten years whereas each of the six biggest economies in the world ten years ago has grown more slowly than the world average. Today the average Indian is twice as well off as ten years ago while the average Japanese or German is barely better off at all. China's GDP has more than doubled relative to that of the United States in the last twenty-five years. Taking a longer period, the growth rates of the poorest fifth of countries (the poorest quintile) from 1950 to 2001 was not significantly different from those of the other 80 percent of countries.[13]

It is important, too, to place these advances within the context of the long span of world economic history. For nearly the whole of that history until 1800, about 80 percent of the world's population lived on a subsistence income or below. Then, in 1800, the first phase of globalization began and, after 150 years, the proportion of the world's population living in dire poverty halved. In the second phase of globalization, beginning in 1980, the proportion of the world's population living in dire poverty halved again—this time in just twenty-five years.[14] These achievements, resulting from the extension of the market economy based on free economic exchange (or at least freer economic exchange) and the expansion of global trade, have been immense. The reduction in the proportion of the world's population living in absolute poverty has come at a time when the world's population has been expanding. Indeed, the analyst who documented the remarkable advances against poverty believes that the figures on which he bases his findings understate the true improvement in poverty rates and this would seem to be confirmed by recent work by other scholars.[15] Also notable is the expansion of the global middle class in the recent phase of globalization.[16] This is important because there has been huge growth in the number of people in formerly very poor countries who are able to afford not just the necessities of life but also consumer durables and other luxury items while having some income left over to save. For example:

[13] William Easterly, "Reliving the '50s: The Big Push, Poverty Traps and Takeoffs in Economic Development," Center for Global Development, Working Paper No. 65, 2005.

[14] Daniel Griswold, *Mad About Trade: Why Main Street America Should Embrace Globalization* (Washington, D.C.: Cato Institute, 2009).

[15] See Maxim Pinkovskiy and Xavier Sala-i-Martin, "African Poverty is Falling ... Much Faster Than You Think!" NBER Working Paper 15775, 2010.

[16] See Dilip K. Das, "Globalization and an Emerging Global Middle Class," *Economic Affairs* 29 (September 2009): 89–92.

- In recent years, 70 million people each year have been entering the income band from $6,000 to $30,000 per annum.
- The global middle class is likely to expand to include over 1 billion now-poor people in developing countries over the next twenty years.
- Defining "middle class" at a lower level of income—those earning between $2 a day and $13 a day—the middle class rose from 33 percent of the world's population in 1990 to 49 percent in 2005 (this implies 1.2 billion people pulled out of poverty, mostly in countries that have embraced globalization).

It should be added that as well as material living standards, measures of life expectancy, literacy, infant mortality, and more or less every other measure of wellbeing are all improving.[17]

In very recent years, concern has been expressed about the impact of the commodity boom on those very poor countries that were net importers of food and commodities. Soon after, the impact of the financial crash, it was argued, was likely to affect poor countries to a greater extent than rich countries. Indeed, in various homilies and other statements, Pope Benedict brought this problem to the world's attention. Whatever happened in the very short term, however, does not seem to have seriously affected growth in the medium term. The current World Bank forecast for economic growth in "developing" economies from 2010 to 2012 is between 5.7 percent and 6.2 percent—around three times the forecast for developed countries. With few exceptions, good internal policy is the engine of growth.

As noted above with respect to the concept of relative poverty, sweeping statements about the widening disparity between rich and poor can miss an important subtlety. It is possible for the gap between the richest and poorest to become greater while

---

[17] See Johan Norberg, *In Defence of Global Capitalism* (New South Wales, Australia: Center for Independent Studies, 2005).

the number of poor shrinks, perhaps dramatically. Indeed, this is what has happened. In the last fifty years, many previously poor countries have become much better off. In recent years, many people in some formerly very poor countries, containing around one-third of the world's population, have become better off. The living standards in all the countries that have developed in the last fifty years are still rising more rapidly than living standards in the historical developed world.

Nevertheless, there are some parts of the world, particularly countries in Africa, that have not experienced economic growth adequate to make progress toward eliminating absolute poverty. The number of such underdeveloped countries is declining, thanks to the global economic developments described above. Still, to Christians who adhere to the teachings concerning the universal destination of goods and the preferential option for the poor, existence of any such misery is intolerable. In discussions below, we will address the kinds of measures that might be helpful in overcoming this intransigent poverty. For now, we conclude by reiterating the point that many previously poor countries have grown richer even if the gap between the very richest and the very poorest has grown. This observation allows us to understand better the conditions for successful development. It is a better starting point for constructive analysis than the unqualified presumption that income disparities are widening.

VI The Economics of Aid

If poverty is falling in many countries, it leads to the questions of why that is so and whether aid helps the process of development and leads to reductions in poverty. If government-to-government aid of the sort implicitly or explicitly promoted in some papal encyclicals and by local bishops' conferences and Catholic agencies is to be championed, then it must be shown to be beneficial to those whom it is supposed to help. In short, development aid should be proved to be, on balance, supportive of development.

Yet, there is a substantial body of evidence that indicates just the opposite. The arguments and evidence will not be discussed in detail here, but a prima facie case will be made that development aid can be harmful and that the case for development aid is weak. This is not to say that assistance given through charity might not be helpful to poor communities even if government aid is not: Development aid given through political structures has different characteristics for various reasons. Those who insist that development aid remains a desirable feature of economic policy need to challenge this argument or come up with methods of distributing aid that will circumvent the problems discussed here. The summary of problems with government aid that are presented here draw on the much more extensive work of a coterie of scholars working in the field.[18]

The Bauer Critique of Papal Encyclicals

Economist Peter Bauer (d. 2002) was critical of various aspects of the social encyclicals relating to the concentration of wealth and development aid.[19] From *Populorum Progressio* (1967), for example, Bauer quotes and calls into question passages such as "God intended the earth and all that it contains for the use of every human being and people" (PP, no. 22) and "You are not making a gift of your possessions to the poor person. You are handing over to him what is his. For what has been given in common for the use of all, you have arrogated to yourself. The world is given to all, and not only to the rich" (PP, no. 23).[20] On government economic planning, Bauer cites number 33 of the same encyclical: "It pertains to the public authorities to choose, even to lay down, the objectives to be pursued in economic development, the ends to be achieved, and the means of attaining them, and it is for them to stimulate all the forces engaged in this common activity." Bauer then quotes another document from Paul VI, *Octogesima Adveniens* (1971) as stating that there is a major inadequacy in "the fairness in the exchange of goods and in the division of wealth between countries."

Bauer raises some important issues. In particular, it is certainly possible that the tone of *Populorum Progressio* and *Octogesima*

---

18 See, for example, Deepak Lal, "The Poverty of 'Development Economics,'" Hobart Paper 144, Institute of Economic Affairs, London, 2002; Peter Bauer, *From Subsistence to Exchange and Other Essays*, (Princeton, N.J.: Princeton University Press: 2000); Frederik Erixon "Poverty and Recovery: The History of Aid and Development in East Africa," *Economic Affairs* 23 (December 2003): 27–33; Frederik Erixon, *Aid and Development: Will it Work This Time?* (London: International Policy Network, 2005); and Dambisa Moyo, *Dead Aid: Why Aid Is Not Working and How There Is Another Way for Africa* (New York: Farrar, Straus, and Giroux, 2009).

19 See Peter Bauer, "Ecclesiastical Economics: Envy Legitimized," in *From Subsistence*, 94–108.

20 The passage is originally from Saint Ambrose.

Adveniens have abetted the arguments of many leading figures in the Christian community who have proposed wholesale reform of capitalist economies, international trade, financial institutions, aid policies, and so on as the solution to problems of poverty. There is no question that the pursuit of these "solutions" has made poor countries poorer. Bauer also argues that the encyclicals have given succor to those who argue that the rich become rich *at the expense* of the poor.

Father Rodger Charles, SJ, in turn, has criticized Bauer's analysis. Charles points out that Catholic teaching does emphasize that the burden of development belongs with underdeveloped nations themselves. He then suggests that Bauer's critique is inappropriate because he is unable to provide a fully argued case showing how underdeveloped nations can achieve development themselves without help from the outside. He thus suggests that Bauer effectively argued that the popes, and the experts on whom they relied, were wrong, but never articulated "the right."[21]

Charles' critique of Bauer also makes some valid points. Still, Charles' treatment leaves an open question. If a country is poor because its basic economic, legal, and political structures do not allow economic and political freedom to give rise to human flourishing, might it be possible that little can be done through political systems external to the country concerned to rectify this situation? It is perfectly reasonable for academics to point out that proposed solutions to particular problems will do more harm than good while still being unable, themselves, to resolve the problems.

As we have noticed, over time, papal encyclicals have seemingly become more sensitive to the dangers of aid and to the potential of the market economy than was *Populorum Progressio*. Whereas *Populorum* argued that in good conscience we must support policies of higher taxes to finance aid—a notion strongly criticized by Bauer—John Paul II's *Solicitudo Rei Socialis* was

---

[21] Charles, *Christian Social Witness*, 455–56.

more nuanced. It might be better to infer from the later writings that *if we know how* to alleviate poverty and choose not to do so, this is a moral failing.[22] In other words, the pope stipulates that the imputation of moral guilt occurs when we know how poverty may be mitigated yet fail to act. In this formulation, the question of how poverty can be most effectively addressed remains open to debate. If development depends exclusively or primarily on the reformation of political structures and culture within an underdeveloped nation, then there may be little that wealthier nations can accomplish in this cause. Bauer's belief that the developed world does not have it in its power to resolve the problems of the underdeveloped world would not contradict the sentiments of *Solicitudo rei socialis.*

Aid in Theory and Practice

Although few economists have followed Bauer by taking on papal encyclicals directly, many other researchers on foreign aid have had much to say about the efficacy—or otherwise—of foreign aid, and this research is also relevant to our discussion. There are a number of ways in which the provision of government aid can be damaging to its recipients.

Aid and Government

The provision of government development aid is, by nature, a top-down process. At a fundamental level, therefore, aid rewards the governing elite in those countries where those in power keep their people poor. Aid also makes it more likely that incompetent, corrupt, or brutal government will survive because aid provides the resources for the elite to alleviate some of the internal problems caused by poor or unjust governments. Frequently, such governments have pursued policies that involve the persecution or expulsion of the most productive

---

[22] I am grateful to Fr. Raymond de Souza, Kingston, Ontario, Canada for this insight.

ethnic groups in society. The availability of aid also provides incentives for governments to pursue policies that will attract more aid—that is, policies that lead to high levels of absolute poverty and policies that promote government consumption and not investment, thus giving the impression that money is not available for investment, health, and education.

Aid also changes lines of accountability in government. Governments become accountable to those from whom they receive aid—either other governments or international institutions—and not to their own people. In 2001, Tanzania had to produce 2,400 reports and studies on different aspects of present and future aid. A former minister of finance of Kenya estimated he had to spend 75 percent of his time in discussions with donors.[23]

As Bauer pointed out, development aid leads a country's political and economic structures to orientate themselves inappropriately. In many African countries, aid is a significant proportion of national income.[24] Talented and entrepreneurial people within a country that receives large amounts of aid have a strong incentive to direct their efforts upward, toward government, to become beneficiaries of aid-financed projects, instead of attempting to raise their material position through business and entrepreneurship. Thus, aid encourages what economists call *rent seeking*, whereby work is directed toward collecting government largesse rather than toward producing goods and services that benefit the human community. This whole process strengthens the hold of government on economic life, which is generally one of the most serious problems in underdeveloped countries.

On a wider scale, the greater the proportion of national income and wealth that is controlled by government, the greater is the incentive for ethnic groups to engage in conflict to try

---

[23] Erixon, "Poverty and Recovery."
[24] In Tanzania and Kenya, for example, it reached 30 percent of national income in the mid 1990s.

to control government. In contrast, if freedom of contract, exchange, and private property rights are the main vehicles for transferring and upholding the control of property, fruitful economic activity, rather than political activity and conflict, are more likely to produce increases in income and wealth for individuals and communities.

The negative relationship between economic growth and natural resources is now well established: the so-called natural resource curse.[25] In economic terms, the provision of aid is very much like the existence of natural resources within a country: Aid is an "endowment" which empowers governments and makes it more worthwhile to invest economic resources or even to use military means to control the machinery of government. Aid can therefore nurture bad government, which is the very problem that entrenches poverty in the first place. Studies have found a strongly negative relationship between the receipt of aid and the extent of democracy.[26]

There is also a tendency for aid not to be used for its intended purpose, such as health and education but, instead, to be used to meet the aims of the governing elite (often including personal betterment). This can happen for two reasons. First, aid might be siphoned off before it reaches its intended recipients. A 2004 survey tracked spending, by the government of Chad, that had been intended for rural hospital projects. Only 1 percent of the money intended for the projects actually reached the hospitals. It is therefore not surprising that about 40 percent of Africa's military spending is inadvertently financed by aid.[27] This should be a striking revelation for religious leaders and others who advocate generous government aid while simultaneously decrying the arms trade and violence that plague many African nations.

---

[25] See Jeffrey D. Sachs and Adrew M. Warner, "The Curse of Natural Resources," *European Economic Review* 45 (May 2001): 827–38.

[26] Simeon Djankov, Jose Garcia-Montalvo, and Marta Reynal-Querol, "Does Foreign Aid Help?" *The Cato Journal* 26 (March 2006): 1–28.

[27] Reported in Peter Collier, *The Bottom Billion: Why the Poorest Countries Are Failing and What Can Be Done About It* (Oxford: Oxford University Press, 2007).

Another problem is that aid is "fungible."[28] The specific aid money directed toward investment in health and education may be used for the intended purposes in order to provide evidence for donors. However, this aid money displaces investment that otherwise would have taken place in such sectors, including private sector investment. The additional resources are then, in effect, used for government consumption.

If aid is diverted in either of these two ways, it reinforces the drawbacks identified above: the government becomes more dominant in economic life and the source of economic betterment. The increased resources enhance the ability of government to pursue active industrial policies with the usual detrimental effects. Increased resources also find their ways into the hands of the governing elite and their supporters. In summary, aid entrenches the position of those who are rich and powerful and encourages individuals who wish to improve their economic position to do so by developing relationships with those responsible for the spending of aid.

All of these problems promote corruption in public life. If development aid receipts are a significant proportion of national income, then the resources available to government are greater. In such situations, government functionaries and ministers have relatively more power and economic resources that can be used for economic preferment. Government officials and politicians are in a position where they control the allocation of substantial economic resources and therefore become more susceptible to corruption, particularly where legal systems are inadequate or are themselves corrupt.[29]

---

[28] See Erixon, *Aid and Development*, 11.

[29] This should not be thought a patronizing remark about the governments of underdeveloped countries (see Ian Senior, *Corruption—The World's Big C*, IEA Research Monograph No. 61, July 2006; available at www.iea.org.uk). In any country where government officials have control of vast economic resources and significant discretion, fraud and corruption are likely to result (witness the EU Common Agricultural Policy). However, if countries are already poor because of bad governance, providing development aid can simply feed the system that keeps the country poor.

These political problems also infect the donor countries. If donor country charities, NGOs, and consultants are the channels of significant amounts of aid funds, they have an incentive to campaign for aid-financed solutions to poverty in underdeveloped countries (see discussion of CAFOD above).

In an ideal world, the provision of aid might simply work to raise the income of all poor people in a country by an equal amount. People living at subsistence levels would then have more money to save, invest, and provide education and health care for their families. However, aid does not work like this, partly because it comes from governments of donor countries and is spent through governments of recipient countries, leading to the effects described above. However, it is also not symmetrical in its effect on different economic sectors.

This is especially the case, paradoxically, when aid is spent wisely. For example, if aid is spent on investment projects, it can lower the marginal rate of return from investment projects financed by private saving and thus reduce private saving and investment. In any event, aid will raise the real rate of exchange in a country, thus reducing the competitiveness of export sectors.[30] Other nonexport-orientated sectors may benefit, of course, but any structural adjustment caused by significant changes in aid may cause problems for particular sectors of the economy.

---

[30] This may seem like an esoteric point, but a research paper (Raghuram G. Rajan and Arvind Subramanian, "What Undermines Aid's Impact on Growth," NBER Working Paper No. 11657, National Bureau of Economic Research, U.S., 2006) suggests that it can be of fundamental importance, particularly if aid flows are considerable in a country that has had little development. Gupta, Powell, and Yang provide a good discussion of these issues. They note that trade liberalization should coincide with increases in aid to reduce the impact of the "real exchange rate effect"; Sanjeev Gupta, Robert Powell, and Yongzheng Yang, *Macroeconomic Challenges of Scaling Up Aid to Africa: A Checklist for Practitioners* (Washington, D.C.: International Monetary Fund, 2006). Pattillo, Gupta, and Carey note that this effect can be most detrimental to the poor, though they also suggest that it can be avoided through good policy choices in other areas; Catherine Patillo, Sanjeev Gupta, and Kevin Carey, *Sustaining and Accelerating Pro-Poor Growth in Africa* (Washington, D.C.: International Monetary Fund, 2006).

Both supporters and opponents of aid agree that policies to tie aid to economic reform have not succeeded where economic reform is initiated by the funding body.[31] There are many reasons for this. It is too easy for countries to demonstrate, at the time that grants or loans tied to structural adjustment are being renewed, that progress has been made—even though progress is more apparent than real. Additionally, lenders and donors find it very difficult not to renew loans or grants if a country has become poorer because economic reform policies have not been followed.

Aid and Development

A strong economic case for aid rests on two assumptions. The first is that the preconditions for economic development and growth relate to a shortage of savings, problems caused by declining terms of trade, lack of education, and so on, which can be resolved by income transfers from rich to poor countries. The second is that, in practice, aid transfers can be managed by benign governments that can resolve these problems. We have made a prima facie case that these conditions might not hold. What does the empirical work say about aid and development?

It is, in fact, hard to find a positive relationship between aid and growth: Indeed, there appears to be a negative relationship. It does not follow that a negative relationship between aid and economic growth necessarily implies cause and effect, but it does, at least, call into question unqualified exhortations to increase aid. It also renders problematic any suggestion that support for government aid should be considered a moral imperative.

After the late 1970s, aid to Africa grew rapidly, yet GDP growth collapsed and was close to zero or negative for over a decade beginning in 1984.[32] GDP growth in Africa did not start to pick up again until aid fell in the early to mid 1990s. In East

---

[31] See Erixon, *Aid and Development*, and the references therein.

[32] Erixon, *Aid and Development*.

Asia, South Asia, and the Pacific, one finds a similar trend. As aid was reduced in these regions from the early 1990s, national income increased rapidly. A number of detailed country studies find no benefits from aid whatsoever across a range of periods and a large number of countries. In total, in the thirty years after 1970, Africa received $400bn of aid, under different regimes, tied to different forms of economic policy and reform, yet there is no evidence of a single country developing because of aid.[33]

If we take 1950 as a starting point, it is clear that many countries that were then poor have become relatively wealthy while others have remained poor. It is impossible to find evidence that aid was an important factor in helping those countries that have become rich. Botswana, for example, increased its income per head thirteenfold from 1950 to 2001 while much of Africa had a zero or negative growth rate.[34] This progress is almost certainly due to Botswana possessing many of the important features of good governance. Differences in aid do not distinguish Botswana from other African countries.

The following two figures show the relationship between aid and economic growth (figure 1) and aid and improvements in life expectancy (figure 2).[35] It is very clear that there is no statistically significant relationship in either case. This is not because aid tends to be focused on the countries that are growing slowly, as more detailed econometric studies show. The data suggest strongly that aid does not improve either economic growth or important human development indicators such as mortality.

---

[33] See Erixon, *Aid and Development*.

[34] Easterly, "Reliving the '50s."

[35] The author thanks Julian Morris for supplying these figures.

Figure 1

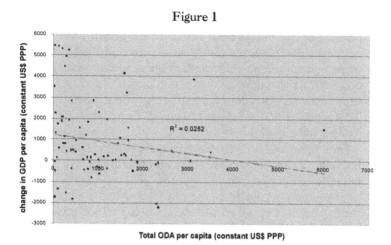

Overseas Development Aid and Change in GDP per Capita
(1975–2000)

Figure 2

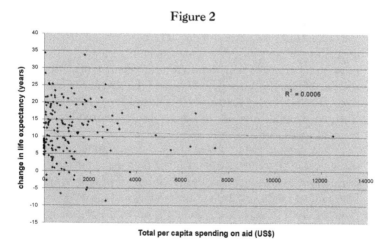

Overseas Development Aid and Change in Life Expectancy

A final important point stems from the fact that around 40 percent of the poorest one-fifth of countries in 1985 were not among the poorest one-fifth of countries in 1950.[36] Thus, while most attention is focused on the challenge of assisting poor countries to develop, it is also the case that nations can experience negative development (at least in relative terms). This suggests that aid is not the crucial factor affecting a nation's economic well-being.

From these observations, three facts are clear: (1) poor countries can develop without aid, (2) countries that receive aid do not tend to develop, and (3) countries that are relatively rich can become poor again. These phenomena are troubling for the hypothesis that aid overcomes lack of capital and promotes development. The evidence suggests that good internal policy drives economic development and growth.

Growth and Governance

It is becoming increasingly clear both from studying countries that have developed (for example, in Asia) and those that have not, that the problems identified by aid proponents are not the crucial ones for development. The basic preconditions for development are good governance, including the protection of private property, freedom of contract, enforcement of contracts, the rule of law, the authority of law, and the absence of corruption. This list is not exhaustive, of course.[37] Yet, it appears that if these preconditions are present, development and growth will usually follow.

This is not surprising. Economic activity, employment, saving, and capital accumulation will not take place unless there is freedom of contract and enforcement of property rights. Hernando de Soto's analysis of developing nations in *Mystery of Capital* (2000) treats in great detail the problems caused by the

---

[36] Easterly, "Reliving the '50s."
[37] One could add fiscal prudence and sound money, for example.

absence of formalization and the security of property rights.[38] De Soto argues that in underdeveloped countries much capital is "dead capital" that is not recognized by the legal system. The absence of both secure and formal property rights prevents proper business contracts from developing, leads to reduced opportunities for entrepreneurship, prevents capital secured on property from being invested within businesses, leads to corrupt legal and governmental systems, and leads to private law enforcement or so-called mafia gangs becoming dominant. In such a situation, issues such as land reform and the provision of capital through aid become irrelevant to development. Unless legal systems are reformed to properly recognize freely acquired property, capital investment and land endowments for the poor will have no meaning and will not contribute to development.

Exchange relationships are clearly necessary for an economy to develop beyond subsistence level. If contracts are not enforceable in the courts or recognized by legal systems, or if corruption or violence leads them to be enforced perversely, then exchange relationships cannot develop. Similarly, if property rights are not enforced justly or are not recognized, only very limited capital investment can take place.

It is sometimes difficult for people in the West, who tend to take these preconditions for granted, to understand the importance of this point. If contracts that one makes as a consumer, employee, businessperson, or employer are not enforceable (including contracts for borrowing and saving), business life simply cannot thrive. Similarly, if one cannot enforce property rights in one's house, land, or business premises, capital investment will grind to a halt.

The problems with developing exchange relationships, small businesses, and entrepreneurship are well illustrated both by De Soto's findings and by regular reports by the World Bank

---

[38] Hernando de Soto, *The Mystery of Capital: Why Capitalism Triumphs in the West and Fails Everywhere Else* (London: Black Swan, 2000).

and the Economist Intelligence Unit. For example, De Soto shows how on average, 15 percent of turnover in Peruvian manufacturing businesses were paid out in bribes. For a business to become legal and register its property in Lima, it took over three hundred working days at a cost of thirty-two times the monthly minimum wage. A person living in a housing settlement where the title was not formally registered had to go through 728 individual bureaucratic steps to register the title with the city of Lima authority alone.

The World Bank 2010 *Doing Business* report ranks all countries by the ease of doing business. African countries have an average rank of 139 in the world compared with Organisation for Economic Co-operation and Development (OECD) countries that have an average rank of 30. It should be said that African countries are now among the top reformers, and reform certainly translates into higher economic growth, as well as to a safer society. If obstacles to business are too high, one effect is that an exchange economy can descend into a subsistence economy, thus leading to abject poverty. However, difficulties in registering businesses can also increase opportunities for brutal exploitation. If a business cannot easily register, it may pay bribes to officials, thus corrupting public life. It will also mean that employees, customers, and suppliers cannot enforce contracts through the courts (because the contracting entity does not exist according to the law). Contracts in such an environment can be enforced, to put it euphemistically, "privately" (at gunpoint). This creates a miserable quality of life.

The relationship between economic freedom and growth is well documented.[39] One particular statistic is compelling. One hundred countries were studied from 1980 to 2000 and their legal systems rated according to the criteria established by the Fraser Institute's *Economic Freedom of the World* index.

---

[39] See, for example, James Gwartney and Robert Lawson, "What Have We Learned from the Measurement of Economic Freedom," in *The Legacy of Milton and Rose Friedman's* Free to Choose, ed. Mark Wynne, Harvey Rosenblum, and Robert Formaini (Dallas, Tex.: Federal Reserve Bank, 2004).

The top twenty-four countries had an average GDP per capita of $25,716 at the end of the period and average economic growth of 2.5 percent. The bottom twenty-one countries had an average income of $3,094 per capita and average economic growth of 0.33 percent. The criteria used to rank legal systems were: consistency of legal structure, protection of property rights, enforcement of contracts, independence of judiciary, and rule-of-law principles. This suggests that development is impossible without the basic legal structures necessary for free economic activity.

There are important subtleties in this debate that admittedly must be taken into account.[40] For example, it could be argued that legal systems are less effective at enforcing property rights and contracts in poor countries because such countries lack the resources to develop effective legal systems. This argument may have some validity but is problematic as a generalization because it raises the question of how any country manages to develop. That is, if some level of wealth is a necessary prerequisite to further development, then how did any nation ever reach that initial, indispensable level of wealth? Also, it would seem that this argument should not apply to resource-rich, underdeveloped countries, of which there are many in Africa.

Scholars studying the sustained economic changes in growth in African countries have identified the critical factors in development, confirming the foregoing discussion. They found that the macroeconomic environment (inflation, government borrowing, and so on) was important—and many of the countries with improved macroeconomic environments were part of Inter-national Monetary Fund (IMF) programs. Economic and political liberalization were important, too, as was trade liberalization. Aid and debt concessions helped long-term growth only when combined with an otherwise healthy policy environment.[41]

---

[40] See the discussion in Anthony Ogus, "Towards Appropriate Institutional Arrangements for Regulation in Less Developed Countries," Paper No. 119, Center for Regulation and Competition, University of Manchester, UK, 2005.

[41] Pattillo, Gupta, and Carey, *Sustaining and Accelerating.*

Summary

The discussion in this chapter is neither conclusive nor comprehensive. However, it provides a prima facie case against government-provided development aid. Those who make the case for government aid need to demonstrate how these problems are either irrelevant or can be overcome. Furthermore, those who promote government development aid in the name of Church teaching should be cautious when implying that the teaching has moral backing. If development aid is damaging to the very people it is meant to help, it is difficult to see how its provision can be a moral requirement.

Insofar as there was a consensus among economists in the 1960s behind the economic theories that were implicit in *Populorum Progressio*, that consensus is now broken. Aid has not been successful in achieving its goals, and it has now become clear why this is so. Economists still disagree on policies relating to the appropriate extent of government intervention in any developing country, and they will always do so. However, it has become clear that development without those aspects of good governance necessary for enterprise is impossible. It is also clear that, if the basics of good governance exist, countries will tend to escape from poverty. Furthermore, one of the effects of aid is that it may well undermine good governance. If that is the case, its provision could be seriously damaging.

It is therefore at least possible that aid does little good and that it may do much harm. Indeed, as Bauer suggested, if aid does the damage its opponents suspect (by entrenching the power of bad government and undermining bottom-up development), the harm that it does is serious. However, if aid has the benefits that its proponents suggest, the evidence indicates that, at best, those benefits are marginal. The strategy that would potentially do least harm to underdeveloped countries would therefore be not to support government-provided development aid.

London School of Economics professor Peter Boone summarizes the difficulty confronting government-aid advocates. He writes: "Only a fraction of this [UK aid] money goes to extremely poor regions, and a fraction of that to areas where we have clear scientific evidence that it could help reduce poverty." Specifically with respect to education assistance, Boone observes that aid cannot solve the endemic problems that require local solutions. "Even the poorest regions of Africa have some kind of school," he notes, "and they probably have a teacher assigned to them. But the schools often do not function."[42]

Thus, neither the theoretical nor the empirical case for foreign aid looks strong. The Holy Father was right to warn us in *Caritas in Veritate* that old models of delivering aid need reappraisal. It is certainly a matter for judgment whether new models can do any better, and it can never be a moral imperative to support a policy that, in practice, harms its intended beneficiaries.

---

[42] Peter Boone, "Making the UK's Aid Budget Work Better," *CentrePiece* (Summer 2010): 3–7.

VII   Conclusion

The mix of charity and political action that is appropriate in order to help the poor is not something the Church generally lays down, and proponents of aid should be careful about drawing conclusions that ignore this tenet when using Catholic teaching to justify their position: "For the Church does not propose economic and political systems or programs, nor does she show preference for one or the other, provided that human dignity is properly respected and promoted, and provided she herself is allowed the room she needs to exercise her ministry in the world" (SRS, no. 41).

The cry that is frequently made by Catholic bishops and agencies for the provision of government development aid in the name of justice is not to be rejected lightly. However, we must ask whether it is within the power of a donor government to put in place the processes of good governance that could allow government aid to help meet the basic needs of the poor and assist the process of development. At the same time, if it were within the power of potential donor governments to create systems of good governance in underdeveloped countries, aid may well not be needed to nurture development. It is certainly a moral failing if we know how to alleviate poverty and do not do so; Christians should, of course, strive to find solutions to these difficult problems. However, it cannot be a moral failing to reject a particular approach to the problem of dire poverty in poor countries based on an honest interpretation of the evidence and theory.

It may be possible to develop ways to distribute aid better so that the problems described above do not arise. Analyst Frederick Erixon posits that aid can complement an internal reform program that is already developing within a country, though aid tied to a reform program imposed from outside does not seem to be effective.[43] Others have suggested that aid could be given if there were an *established* record of reform.[44] Anthony Ogus' study might be regarded as implying that aid could be useful to help develop appropriate legal frameworks that nurture economic development.[45] However, Ogus also points out the difficulty of transplanting a particular model of legal system into other cultures; there is much discussion of this issue in many contexts.[46] The precise form of legal systems, norms for enforcing contracts, recognition of property rights, and so on, will often be culture-specific and may have to evolve within that culture.

There is increasingly widespread recognition of the deficiencies of traditional aid models and the need for new strategies in combating underdevelopment. The report of the United Kingdom's Commission for Africa assimilates some of the points made above and makes clear the importance of governance and trade for growth. The G8 Paris Declaration on Aid Effectiveness also addresses these issues.[47] More generally, much is made of the desire for "smarter" aid. There is a growing desire to ensure that aid should be a complement to internal policies to promote growth. In a sense, this follows recent Catholic social teaching on development and, as has been noted, *Caritas in Veritate* makes

---

[43] Erixon, *Aid and Development*, 19–22.

[44] Pattillo, Gupta, and Carey, *Sustaining and Accelerating*.

[45] Ogus, "Institutional Arrangements."

[46] See, for example, Karol Boudreaux and Paul Aligica, "Paths to Property," Hobart Paper, Institute of Economic Affairs, London, 2007.

[47] *Our Common Interest*, Report of the Commission for Africa, United Kingdom, 2005; *Paris Declaration on Aid Effectiveness*, Organization for Economic Cooperation and Development, 2005.

many wise points about the failings of traditional ways of providing development aid. However, whether it is possible to deliver aid while guaranteeing that other reforms will take place and while not creating incentives for the adoption of bad internal policies is a subjective and pragmatic question. Furthermore, for the reasons stated above, the history of promoting growth by "blueprint" and "planning" from outside is not a happy one, even if the proposed policies have been sound.

Meanwhile, some have undertaken innovative approaches that try to take into account what experience has taught. For example, bottom-up style approaches to providing development assistance are being attempted through the U.S. African Development Foundation (USADF). It provides small grants directly to community groups. The USADF appraises projects and has strict selection criteria. Insofar as it is successful, this success may well result from its small size and thus have few lessons for the provision of development aid more generally. Successful niche approaches to providing development assistance are notoriously difficult to scale.

Government aid provided through the private sector, charities, or agencies might well avoid some of the pitfalls of government-to-government aid. However, as has been noted, it can lead to the politicization of charities and NGOs. A more effective way to deal with this problem might be to replace government aid with more generous tax relief provided to charities.

It may be possible to provide aid more effectively if it is given, for example, directly to the poor to help them pay for education and health care or used to finance the infrastructure of microfinance projects. Microfinance projects can be helpful in providing certain financial services that are lacking, for various reasons, in poor countries. However, we should be wary of generalizing from the success of charitable projects that are effective in this regard by calling for such projects to be repeated on a large scale financed by government aid. The success of particular projects is often a result of particular time, place, circumstances, and people, and these successes cannot simply be scaled up and replicated. Such projects often depend on a subtle mix of charity, reciprocity, and commercial aspects.

These successes do point to the wisdom of various guidelines, however, such as those articulated by Pope Benedict and already mentioned above: "Aid programs must increasingly acquire the characteristics of participation and completion from the grass roots" (CV, no. 58). While this is an important characteristic of charitable assistance, there is a serious question as to whether government aid programs can, on a sustained basis, acquire those characteristics—with the exception of niche programs such as USADF. Perhaps it would be better to provide the conditions whereby charities and other private providers of assistance to underdeveloped countries flourish more easily.

Many of these issues are clearly understood and implicit in much of Catholic social teaching. However, if we accept the economic case against aid, it has implications for the specific exhortations that have been made in social encyclicals on the issue of development. Paragraph 47 of *Populorum Progressio* suggested that individuals in good conscience should not just support projects to help the needy at their own expense but must also support the raising of taxes so that public authorities could expand their work in this area. It is difficult to justify such statements given the empirical and theoretical knowledge we now have on the record of development aid. Some Catholics in good conscience might support increased taxpayer support for aid; others, equally in good conscience, might not. Given that experience of successful development strategies imposed or even nurtured from outside a given country is relatively limited, the specific guidance that it would be reasonable for the Church to give ought to be correspondingly cautious.

Some of the problems that we have described with regard to aid also exist when government-to-government relief is given in times of particular need due to famine and other disasters. Despite this, the arguments favoring caution and nonintervention in such circumstances are weaker. First, if there is a certain and immediate need to be met, then the potential and less certain long-term consequences have less relevance to the decision to provide assistance. Second, it is easier for governments to provide disaster relief using nongovernment agencies in the recipient country, thus, to an extent, avoiding the problem of the aid process entrenching bad governance. By its nature, such assistance is temporary—or should be temporary—and thus has fewer implications for the long-term policy environment.

Our main focus has been on government aid to underdeveloped countries. Charity, provided through bodies that are genuinely independent of political systems in both donor and recipient countries, is less likely to cause harm and may well do much good, even when administered in countries with corrupt and unjust regimes. Many of the problems with government-to-government aid do not apply to charity administered through voluntary agencies, particularly where those voluntary agencies administer assistance through well-established structures in recipient countries that provide not just money but personal ministering to the poor. It is important to point out that we should not wait for a just ordering of the world or good governance in recipient countries before supporting such organizations. A number of statements made in Pope Benedict XVI's first encyclical, *Deus Caritas Est*, stress the importance of charitable action by Christians, *regardless of the underlying causes of the need they are trying to meet.* Pope Benedict states that whether a just society exists here and now is irrelevant to our mission of charity: "There is no ordering of the state so just that it can eliminate the need for a service of love" (DCE, no. 28).[48] He also asserts that the exercise of charity is fundamental to the lives of Christians. It is then made clear that Christian charitable activity must be independent of parties and ideologies: It is an extension of the Christian mission of love not to be

---

[48] This can be considered from two perspectives. First, regardless of the political order, there will always be people in need who are deserving of charity. Second, as is made clear by Pope Benedict elsewhere in the encyclical, charity satisfies a deep human need that government bureaucracies distributing financial and material help cannot meet.

put at the service of political goals.[49] Indeed, perhaps those in the Church who promote government aid do so because they think that charity can never be enough. It is therefore a sobering thought that total U.S. philanthropic support for underdeveloped countries is greater than the government aid budgets of all OECD countries put together—and the effect of that philanthropy is rather more positive than the effect of aid.

The duty of Christians to help those in immediate need is clear. This duty is not conditional on the political order, the reason why help is needed, or whether the help leads to some long-run benefit. Some Christians may wish to apply this reasoning to development aid provided by the state. However, aid provided by the state is fundamentally of a different character to that provided by charity, both morally and economically speaking. On the basis of our knowledge of the theory and evidence it is difficult to argue that, with regard to the political agenda, the Church should recommend continuing support for government-to-government development aid. The Church's social teaching offers a wealth of wisdom and moral guidance through its articulation of the principles of solidarity, the universal destination of goods, preferential option for the poor, and subsidiarity. It does well to stress the obligations of the lay faithful to take the issue of how to facilitate development very seriously. In light of the track record of development aid and Church statements on the subject, it seems prudent to advise that future teaching be clearer in its articulation of the fact that this is an issue on which Christians are free to differ about the means by which desirable ends can be achieved. To go further would be to risk promoting policies that, on the balance of evidence, have done more harm than good.

---

[49] This is emphasized twice, in paragraphs 31 and 33. In paragraph 33, it is stated that those involved in the Church's charity "must not be inspired by ideologies aimed at improving the world, but should rather be guided by the faith which works through love."

References

Church Documents with Abbreviations

The following documents are available online at www.vatican.va.

Benedict XVI, *Caritas in Veritate* (2009), CV.

Benedict XVI, *Deus Caritas Est* (2005), DCE.

John Paul II, *Centesimus Annus* (1991), CA.

John Paul II, *Sollicitudo Rei Socialis* (1987), SRS.

Paul VI, *Populorum Progressio* (1967), PP.

Second Vatican Council, *Gaudium et Spes* (1965), GS.

John XXIII, *Mater et Magistra* (1961), MM.

Leo XIII, *Rerum Novarum* (1891), RN.

Other Church and Related Documents

Benedict XVI. "Fighting Poverty to Build Peace," Message of His Holiness Pope Benedict XVI for the Celebration of the World Day of Peace 2009. Available at www.vatican.va.

CAFOD. *Your Guide to the 2010 General Election*. London, UK: CAFOD, n.d.

Catechism of the Catholic Church. London: Geoffrey Chapman, 1994.

Pontifical Council for Justice and Peace. *Compendium of the Social Doctrine of the Church*. London: Continuum, 2005.

United States Conference of Catholic Bishops. *Faithful Citizenship*. Washington, D.C.: USCCB, 2004, 2008. Available at www.usccb.org.

United States Conference of Catholic Bishops. *Questions on Church Teaching and International Assistance*. Washington, D.C.: USCCB, 2009. Available at www.usccb.org.

Books and Articles

Bauer, Peter. *From Subsistence to Exchange and Other Essays*. Princeton, N.J.: Princeton University Press: 2000.

Boone, Peter. "Making the UK's Aid Budget Work Better." *CentrePiece* (Summer 2010): 3–7.

Boudreaux, Karol, and Paul Aligica. "Paths to Property." Hobart Paper, Institute of Economic Affairs, London, 2007. Available at www.iea.org.uk.

Charles, Rodger, SJ, *Christian Social Witness and Teaching: The Catholic Tradition from Genesis to Centesimus Annus*. Gracewing, Leominster, UK: 1998.

Collier, Peter. *The Bottom Billion: Why the Poorest Countries Are Failing and What Can Be Done About It*. Oxford: Oxford University Press, 2007.

Das, Dilip K. "Globalization and an Emerging Global Middle Class, *Economic Affairs* 29 (September 2009): 89–92.

De Soto, Hernando. *The Mystery of Capital: Why Capitalism Triumphs in the West and Fails Everywhere Else*. London: Black Swan, 2000.

Djankov, Simeon, Jose Garcia-Montalvo, and Marta Reynal-Querol. "Does Foreign Aid Help?" *The Cato Journal* 26 (March 2006): 1–28.

Easterly, William. "Reliving the '50s: The Big Push, Poverty Traps and Takeoffs in Economic Development." Centre for Global Development, Working Paper Number 65, 2005.

Erixon, Frederik. "Poverty and Recovery: The History of Aid and Development in East Africa," *Economic Affairs* 23 (December 2003): 27–33.

———. *Aid and Development: Will It Work This Time?* London: International Policy Network, 2005.

Griswold, Daniel. *Mad About Trade: Why Main Street America Should Embrace Globalization*. Washington, D.C.: Cato Institute, 2009.

Gupta, Sanjeev, Robert Powell, and Yongzheng Yang. *Macroeconomic Challenges of Scaling Up Aid to Africa: A Checklist for Practitioners*. Washington, D.C.: International Monetary Fund, 2006.

Gwartney, James, and Robert Lawson. "What Have We Learned from the Measurement of Economic Freedom." In *The Legacy of Milton and Rose Friedman's Free to Choose*. Edited by Mark Wynne, Harvey Rosenblum, and Robert Formaini. Dallas, Tex.: Federal Reserve Bank, 2004.

Lal, Deepak. "The Poverty of 'Development Economics.'" Hobart Paper 144, Institute of Economic Affairs, London, 2002. Available at www.iea.org.uk.

Moyo, Dambisa. *Dead Aid: Why Aid Is Not Working and How There Is Another Way for Africa*. New York: Farrar, Straus and Giroux, 2009.

Norberg, Johan. *In Defence of Global Capitalism*. New South Wales, Australia: Centre for Independent Studies, 2005.

Ogus, Anthony. "Towards Appropriate Institutional Arrangements for Regulation in Less Developed Countries." Paper No. 119, Centre for Regulation and Competition, University of Manchester, United Kingdom, 2005.

Our Common Interest. Report of the Commission for Africa, United Kingdom, 2005.

Paris Declaration on Aid Effectiveness. Organization for Economic Cooperation and Development, 2005.

Patillo, Catherine, Sanjeev Gupta, and Kevin Carey. *Sustaining and Accelerating Pro-Poor Growth in Africa*. Washington, D.C.: International Monetary Fund, 2006.

Pinkovskiy, Maxim, and Xavier Sala-i-Martin. "African Poverty is Falling … Much Faster Than You Think!" NBER Working Paper 15775. National Bureau of Economic Research, United States, 2010.

Rajan, Raghuram G., and Arvind Subramanian. "What Undermines Aid's Impact on Growth," NBER Working Paper No. 11657. National Bureau of Economic Research, United States, 2006.

Sachs, Jeffrey D., and Andrew M. Warner. "The Curse of Natural Resources." *European Economic Review* 45 (May 2001): 827–38.

Senior, Ian. *Corruption—The World's Big C.* Research Monograph No. 61, Institute of Economic Affairs, London, UK. Available at www. iea.org.uk.

Townsend, Nicholas. "Government and Social Infrastructure: A Fourth Way." In *God and Government*. Edited by J. Chaplin and N. Spencer. London: SPCK, 2009.

Wolf, Martin. *Why Globalization Works*. New Haven, Conn.: Yale University Press, 2004.

About the Author

PHILIP BOOTH is Editorial and Programme Director at the Institute of Economic Affairs in London. He also serves as Professor of Insurance and Risk Management at Cass Business School, City University and is a Fellow of Blackfriars Hall, University of Oxford. Booth is a Fellow of the Institute of Actuaries and a Fellow of the Royal Statistical Society. He has previously worked in the investment department at insurance company Axa and as a consultant to the Bank of England. He has also worked on a number of projects developing insurance and finance education in Central and Eastern Europe. Edited and co-authored books include *Christian Perspectives on the Financial Crash*, *Catholic Social Teaching and the Market Economy*, *The Road to Economic Freedom* (a compilation of the works of a number of Nobel Prize winners in economics) and *Investment Mathematics*. Booth is editor of *Economic Affairs* and associate editor of *The British Actuarial Journal* and *Actuarial Annals*.